Surface Displacements

Other books by Sheila Packa

Mother Tongue
Echo & Lightning
Cloud Birds
Migrations
Night Train Red Dust: Poems of the Iron Range

Surface Displacements

Poems from the Three-Way Continental Divide

Sheila Packa

Sheila Packa

Wildwood River Press

Copyright ©2022 Sheila Packa
All rights reserved

ISBN: 978-1-947787-36-0
Library of Congress Control Number: 2022937252

Wildwood River Press
200 Mount Royal Shopping Circle
P.O. Box 3280
Duluth, MN 55803-2633
www.wildwoodriver.com

Cover photo by Sara Pajunen (www.sarapajunen.com)
Book design by Kathy McTavish (www.mctavish.io)

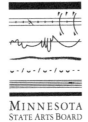

We gratefully acknowledge support for various aspects of this project from the following organizations:

Sheila Packa was a fiscal year 2022 recipient of a Creative Support for Individuals grant from the Minnesota State Arts Board. This activity was made possible by the voters of Minnesota through a grant from the Minnesota State Arts Board, thanks to a legislative appropriation from the arts and cultural heritage fund. She was also a fiscal year 2020 recipient of an Artist Initiative Grant from the Minnesota State Arts Board. This activity is made possible by the voters of Minnesota through a grant from the Minnesota State Arts Board, thanks to a legislative appropriation by the Minnesota State Legislature and by a grant from the National Endowment for the Arts.

Sheila also received an Individual Artist Career Development grant from the Arrowhead Regional Arts Council in 2015. This activity is made possible in part by the voters of Minnesota through a grant from the Arrowhead Regional Arts Council, thanks to appropriations from The McKnight Foundation and the Minnesota State Legislature's general and arts and cultural heritage funds.

This book project, originally titled Three Rivers, was also made possible with the support of a grant in 2016 from Finlandia Foundation National at www.FinlandiaFoundation.org. Finlandia Foundation National invites applications for its grants program, which awards funds to projects related to Finnish-American and Finnish history, heritage, preservation, arts, and culture.

Table of Contents

In the Water
In the Water-Filled Mine Pit 3

Surface Displacements
Surface Displacements 7

Three Rivers
Four Stones 19
Not Drowning 23
Soliloquy 24
Levels 26
Aqua Sienna 28
Breaking 29
Horses 30
Erosions 34
Disappearing Earth 36
Minntac Brand 37
Dialectics 39
Vulture 40
At the Edge 41
Antenna Farm 42
Losing Ground 43
Trace 44
Broken Shell 45
Canadian Geese 48
In the Mind of the Forest 50
Strange Beasts: Boulder Lake 52
Way Finding 54
Snail 55
Blue 56

The Otherworld
Vene / Boat 59

Kieli / Tongue 60
Satama / Harbor 61
Kalevala Viidestoista Runo / Poem 15 62
Rannalla / On the Beach 64
Kääntää / To Translate 65
Katsoa / To Look 66
Hämähäkki / Spider 67
Roukaa / Food 68
Lautasen / Plates 69
Hevonen / Horse 70
Sammal / Moss 71
Mitä Jos Sota / What If a War 72
Kuppi Jäkälä / Cup Lichen 74
Talvi / Winter 75
Sunnuntai / Sunday 76
Revontulet / Aurora Borealis 77
Kengät / Shoes 78

Headwaters

Identity 81
Current 82
Pussywillows 83
No Other Morning like This 84
Weight 85
Names 86
The Dark Season 87
West Two Rivers 88
St. Louis River Route 90
At the Threshold 91
Departure 92
Map / The Way Back 94
Half-Fallen One 96
Luck 97
Yoni 99
Underwater Music 100

Spring 101
A Ghazal: Without Sinking 102
Ode to Where 103
Dawn 104

Coda

Displacements 107
Works Cited 119
Notes 121
Acknowledgments 125
About the Author 128
Wildwood River Press 129

In the Water

In the Water-Filled Mine Pit

In the boat, I slide over her body, the excavation. She is slag. She is crushed stone. Unburied, geologic, Mesabi iron. I drift over knee and shin and float over her shattered self, heaped upon the earth. Over boulders submerged. Veins broken open, emptied and made into freight.

A cold current from the drift. The bow lifts. She is bedrock, the bottom of the continent. Through her runs dark and invisible rivers without shore. She is the Divide. In the seams of the tectonic plates, she is lit with dynamite and extracted, mined, carried by trains to the ships. I see a shoulder of iron. In place of her spine, a deep shaft.

Remade, she becomes steel, becomes bridge, becomes beam. Ship and tank and weapon. At the end, junk in the junkyards rusting into the weeds.

∧

The vessel turns like the needle of a compass broken from its post. I hear the tail splash of a trout. Fish spiral along the perimeter inside the pit. Inside, a winding road once traveled, in shifts, by men in hard hats in dump trucks and steam shovels. The trout tend the broken cables, the skeletal rusted frames.

Stained with ore, the water feels like ice. It rises. Engineers call it water gain: precipitation, surface water inflow, a rise in the water table, a threat to the walls of the pit. Light falls but can't find bottom three hundred feet below. Circles tumble and bend beneath the water's surface. I hear the gravel sliding in. I hear insects and bird wings over the factory of the deep.

∧

Cold blue from afar, the water goes amber. It magnifies the hand that I plunge beneath the surface. It breaks the lines of my body, her body, the vessel. Ore rises into dust, condenses into a red mist of atoms, becomes discharge, industrial contamination. We break the surface. We sink and rise.

Surface Displacements

Surface Displacements

An acre of music or a room closer to it
—Lorine Niedecker

∧

The minerals whisper: iron, manganese,
copper, nickel, platinum, and titanium.
On the Laurentian Divide, one river falls over stones
to Hudson Bay. Another falls south through fields
to the Mississippi. The third river goes east
through the Great Lakes and St. Lawrence Seaway.

∧

Handfuls of water. A body of sea smoke, of wind,
a body of motion, an ocean without salt.
In the benthos, tailings from taconite mines.
In the basin, shipwrecks and broken bottles and sunken
barrels and bodies the lake has claimed.

∧

On a bridge made of paper, my voice turns to vapor.
On a bridge made of iron and steel
I veer between traction and black ice
wander through beams and woven branches
follow the rain in its tracks through roots and excavations.
I cross before, almost, never,
the thunder of interior dialogues
through heavy machinery.

∧

Practicing the old art,
my father once crossed the slope
holding a slender branch, calling the water.

Divining. Now, in a dark room, a daughter holds
a cello to her breast. In the instrument is the old tree.
The wood turns toward harmonics.
The bow rises, glides, floats above the bridge.
Calls of the geese overhead vibrate
against the windowpane. Her fingers tremble
like strings and the water answers.
A car comes down the street. The driver
locked in a dream, rolls down the hill. Slower.
Still. The branch dips and the invisible flows
into containers. The forked branch
didn't know it had lost its root.
It only had yearning.

∧

I call the rivers in the forgotten language
call the Sawtooth Mountains,
forested slopes with snowshoe hares and deer beds
and bears' dens and lynx.
I call shore's perpetual threshold.
In the city, in a house, I call a moth
caught between two panes of glass.
To catch it will damage the wings.
To leave it means it will perish.
I write of the trapped and desperate flight.

∧

No one can follow the map of the bees.
Their business is in every direction,
from tiger lilies into the hives to the chives
to other realms with heads of clover.
Apple blossoms. In the lavender colonnades

of mint through the rooms of June
into purple irises, yellow daylilies, deep inside
delicate tunnels with hardly a foothold
hidden in clouds of pollen.

∧

Along Fourth Street, the rapids climb a bed of stones
amid revelers, but alone
over a steep slope with winter's melt
below a bridge, a bird on a wire, hidden by trees
past a canvas tent and pillow with nobody home.
The constellation of Orion
roams through clouds and goes on a shifting path
with the sleepless river, plunging deep.

∧

A river catches herself as she is falling.
She is a cloud that breaks open and the earth
that holds the seed as it is broken.
The farther she has gone, the closer she comes.
The more she is lost, the more she has found.
Her body is formed by what she touches.
Blind, she sees. Deaf, she hears.
The wind is her breathing. In her emptiness
she fills. In her erasures, she is writing.
The colder the air, the deeper she goes.
The more it rains, the more rain she carries.
The more stones in her path, the more that she laughs.

∧

A blueprint on a scroll of paper: a bridge is built
for floating on air, but heavily, on pylons
wading in plaits of current.

Passengers go between steel cables and arches
and bows, through quicksilver and mercury and yellow.
The homeless meander below.
This bridge, made to join, to cast a permanent shadow.
This bridge, made to resist wind and gravity.
This bridge made, above all, to echo and hum.

∧

Between steel rails on ramps of forward and back
I merge in the traffic. In the union of opposing forces
accelerating through ribs of steel and spider webs.
Once in a dark kitchen, there was an old woman sifting.
The flour falls through the screen.
Once the oil of the lamp climbed a wick
lit a small conflagration above the round oak table
in a circle of chairs, a murmuring, a call for grace.
The roar of a flame mingles with
the chink of forks and knives.
A man, injured in the mine, lies in his bed.
On the bridge, red brake lights. Cars surge
past a blur of years suspended in fine dust.
The bridge sways.
Wheels stir the filaments, litter drifts
where words can't reach.

∧

On foot. On the span, falling without falling.
Say I cross the bridge,
although it is windy and missteps are fatal.
Say clouds cover the moon and I cross borders
without knowing. Say the wind blows at my clothes,
strips me of my protection
and I lose my footing. Say I fall through the night

break through the surface in a cold fire.
Say I vacate — abandon my saying,
withdraw my breath, take my hands from my hands,
twist from my shoulders. Say I walk or am carried
to the place before birth, the place where the sun
comes as a ribbon of heat.
Say I arrive in another language,
wings lifting and landing,
to speak with a wild tongue.

∧

Here, a sketch of shore. The pencil draws
a water line, a vanishing point. In graphite,
wings of a bird in flight. Two more curves,
parabolas that float. Next, between the boat's ribs, a bench.
A wave on the water's surface — not much — just grasses
bent beneath a wind. Then a shadow, three-dimensional.
There's a need to leave things out. In the silence
those that peer uneasily, advance, and then withdraw.
Granite outcroppings — broken by ice.
Already the currents pull and the hull lifts and sways, restless.
I render this as if I were — disembarked —
without a body, without a shadow, a current of air.

∧

Jointed and broken, the skeletal hand raked the beach.
It drifted and reached, five long finger bones bleached
and worn clean. A hand and nothing else.
Was it a bear? A deceased? Wind blew from the northeast.
No other bones to be seen — no other walkers.
Grass was chased over the dunes. Trees leaned
away from the sea. Clouds lifted in each crest.
Pebbles unsettled the bottom, rode through the knuckles

and left no print. The water was sky,
clear and tinted with old blood or rust, rot of fish
and soft ice. Inside were rivers and constellations,
storm wrecks and lives ground into splinters.

∧

In the hollow of the body, a crow comes with a sharp beak.
The door of the chamber opens and closes.
I cannot translate this well. The arteries are open.
There is nothing apparent, the same pressure as always.
Life goes on. The crow grows a long shadow
and takes short flights along low branches.
I walk under the trees when the days are short.
The crow flaps its rough wings and squawks.
This what you call death, she says, I eat.

∧

Here, bulbs are forced to bloom. They are planted
in the ground before winter.
Here, mouths are filled with soil. Those
who entered the tomb and grew roots
and walked in cold layers
to draw the minerals out. Those are the ones
who yield to the shovel and receive the bones,
those are the ones who weave a net and lift the stones.
There are those who seep or are swept
into the underground river, who decay and are kept and yet,
rise in a tender green stem to carry new buds.

∧

I walk over the narrow holes of diamond drillers.
Above the horizon, seagulls draw arcs in flight.
In the morning on shore, sandpipers run on wet sand.

Feathers lift and fall, driven by wind's breath.
I find, half buried in the sand, lost thresholds.
Scrolls of birchbark, small arches, angles
and grayed frames of doors that once opened and closed.

∧

In the city are those who cannot be traced.
In the city of good air and bad are ghost cities,
old cities, cities of war with lamps that no longer burn
but pierce the tongue, cities that write in smoke
in a book open to depredations and
cities that reassemble endings in a dark room
of unknown dimensions, suspend belief,
upend the fields. In the city, I affix the disappeared
to sheets of onion skin with stains and smudges.
Trans-literate. Splice the image.

∧

My hand disappears over the horizon
and pulls up the sea for cover.
I travel as a cloud for miles, citizen of a bruised sky.
I cross the tides to climb the coast
follow roads to the interior
and rivers flow over my banks.
My border spans the continents, and my spine
grows into a mountain range.
My arms can't carry the load.
The cast off, the rejected, the driven
and defenseless. Everywhere they come forth,
everywhere off course.

∧

Seagulls wheel. The hidden drifts.
Freighters and ships embark
in the harbor, trembling with heat,
breathe cold vapor
and speak in the language of horns.
In their wake, the undocumented
travel with currents that carry the vessel.
May it not sink.
May they not be detained or taken by claw or beak
or roll like driftwood on the bottom of the sea
but rise to their feet and climb the beach.

∧

To swing like a branch in a storm
whose edges are accelerating,
to heave with the waves in the slant of hurled rain.
To hear the thump and crack in the too-early dark,
see the electric pour into a hollow.
To find a vein and excavate,
see absences in the landscape.

∧

Strangers come to the edge and double back
because vessels are small and voices can carry,
because children are heavy and nothing is cheap,
because destinations are far and some roads lead nowhere
because fences are one thing and rivers another,
because rocks rise beneath the feet
and holes can be deep, because we look
at the water and don't see any crossings,
because journeys disappear and time erases the map,
because words cloud the distance

between us, because no matter how many have made it
or how many have foundered, they still come,
because what falls from our grasp lands in the past,
because when the wind rises, waves make mountains to climb.

∧

Difficult, to move a border. To clear a forest.
Difficult even to open the furrows
in the field. We lift the seeds and scatter.
If we don't cut every year, the forest will take over.
Imagine a beaver on the sandbar of Lake Superior.
She slides into the surf and emerges
with a piece of driftwood, in that heavy surf,
and lays the first beam of her house.

∧

In the forest, most seeds flung by wind or wings
never sprout. Seedlings compete for the smallest bit of sun.
A white pine, one hundred feet tall,
can be felled by gooseberries.
Slash and burn feeds a coming year's crop of blueberries.
The forest thrives on waste. Dark wings flutter.
A red-headed woodpecker knocks
on the houses of the dead and pulls the worms out.

∧

The center was never a destination.
Inside the fallen trunks are roads — circles around circles.
Insects in the canyons of bark travel with their bundles,
fall into the dark rooms of the camber,
get caught in rivers of sap turning to amber.
Anchored in the rot where so much thrives —
lichen reaches up to sketch on the rocks.

∧
A catbird hidden in the branches
whistles and squeaks and whines and mews.
A catbird says whatever it hears.
Short notes turn into phrases, are repeated.
She can see over the Divide a river of clouds.
She can hear underground, in the rivers that scour the drifts,
a moneyed sound.

Three Rivers

Four Stones

∧

Buried in the earth, held by frost
warmed by the sun
are four wave-worn stones.

Each is an egg
that will never hatch.
Each is a has been.
Each is yet to be.
Each has been delivered.
Each has been born of mineral
born of fire
born of pressure.

The shore has washed
our tracks,
wiped each day.
The shore has no memory
only stones.

∧

In the sound of water
I remember
all the launches we made,
the landings.

Remember my mother's morning task,
the wash.
Her waves in a machine,

the swish and flap of wet
clothes she wrung
and hung on lines,
small stones beneath her feet.

Remember a trip to the cold lake.
We slipped on stones and waded in,
skipped flat stones across
the surface and swam.
Cold water behind the ear drum
trickled from our ears.

Remember the bridge
over the bay,
the beach where
we laid in the sun.

In the sauna, fire roared
in the stove
and heated the round stones.
We sweated
threw more water
that hissed back with steam.
Laid cold cloths on our faces.
Cooled our naked bodies
with buckets of cold lake water
rubbed our peach skin
with rough towels.

Remember betrothals
and births
the baptisms.
The paddle splash and canoe that
broke the waves.

Over the sound of waves
was the sound of birds.

The shore comes up
all the time.
The wind has fallen to nothing.

∧

These stones are time in my hands.
They have been broken by ice.
They've been in an ocean's
embrace and know
the motion that falls and rises.

Stones ride the drift.
Continents fold.
Stones are born of weight.

They remember tectonic plates
the asteroid and endless winter.

A stone can hold even
a bird's tracks. Memory
momentary and heavy.

Each leaves a trace.

The ocean knows the wind's hand
and wind knows
how it can be driven wild by fire.
The stones roll in the sea
that rolls and rolls.

Edges join. The stones round
each other.
Seagulls shriek.

∧
Each stone's weight
isn't always its center.
Each stone feels my hand like a wave.
I stack four in the wind
as if to say, stones have a body.
A body who won't stay.

Not Drowning

I was born into another language, my mother's tongue,
shore to sapphire and stones, music of accordions,
tailgate parties, and night-time arguments.

Instead of beginning, expect hidden sources,
underground springs. A brogue, a Finnish tongue.
I slept in her silences, in the sound of falling water,

learned to swim by drowning.
I poured sentences into waves that rose into crests and broke,
rolled my r's like surf and swallowed the mist, toxic waste,

green organic matter.
This is where I wade, oblivious to the drop-off.
Pebbles ground down to syllables and vowels.

All the same, according to the river, erosion and accretion,
migration and digression.
Now is the river and now and now it's losing ground.

Nothing stops here. And her, she bewilders.
Wilder for a moment, then idler. Ice or vapor.
In shallows or in the deep, meanders.

Asleep in the river, a channel open
goes through violence and its after-wash,
through silence and sibilance and distant acquaintance,

a place to join instead of begin, a place of apprehension,
of tension, of fluid dynamics, all her saying now
under water's music.

Soliloquy

∧

Grandmother poured a shot of brandy into her coffee. *Puna*, she called it. Always an apron and black shoes with thick heels and thin laces. The liquor bottle in the kitchen cabinet, top shelf, on the Iron Range. My grandfather was already gone. In several directions. They migrated from Finland and I was lost in their language. Years later, I learned puna meant red. I learned the word for river, *joki*, sounding like yoke key.

∧

The pendulum clock knocks in the night and strikes the hours with small bells. The chrome kitchen table and yellow Naugahyde chairs listened to the empty rooms, pale green and the carpet, deep green. On the wall, a pastoral: cows heading toward a barn and a horse-drawn wagon on a road, never arriving. Nearby are silhouettes, framed, and a family portrait with my grandfather at the center, passed out near a kerosene stove below a ceiling vent. A television connected to an antenna. Behind its convex glass, interference.

∧

When my mother was small, there were ten children in a two-bedroom house. Too many mouths, not enough hands. Shadows with a long reach. In the hallway, a Singer sewing machine, a pincushion, a basket of unfinished business, wool scraps to make a weighty blanket for the bed. Don't think about the past, my mother said. I was not released. In the kitchen, she stood at a white porcelain sink with cold water only. It drained into a slop bucket behind a white curtain. One must remember to take the bucket out. To wind the clock. To keep the pantry door open so it wouldn't freeze. To leave things out.

∧

No doors inside the house, just curtains with cabbage roses, maroon and pink. Outside the window, a view of clotheslines. In Toivola, the place that meant beautiful, she had an outhouse, a swamp full of tadpoles, and horseflies. Inside, a record player, a stack of 78s and 45s, Hank Williams, Johnny Cash, Patsy Cline. All the children left home early. Crickets. Grasshoppers. Cats.

∧

In the barn, the hay slid into the stalls and hooves knocked on the barn floor. I saw brown bottles of beer and cows' tails tied up with binder twine. This is where the bullets landed. Not in the flesh, only in the wood. If that was his aim. Acres of muskeg. The story was told but not to me. I heard whispers. It was over my head, and I couldn't swim. Nights of lighted tobacco smoke and accordions. On the instruments, bellow clips and register switches. Inside, reeds and wax.

∧

Outside, push and pull. I realize the way my eyes deceive me. I went back, walked on the same ground, looked to the other country, the places where my grandmother left. Why did she leave? Why did she stay? I heard hands playing the instruments, and the sound of falling water. The swish of taffeta slips over secrets. The feet that said, *Unohda!* Forget it. The heels said, *Ei kestä!* Don't mention it.

Levels
for Lake Superior

The lake is blind
when it sings
the song's physics unwind
play on lower registers

under its face are landscapes
settling and unsettling
deep, liquid forests swaying
in a cold fire and weighing

what floats,
what comes ashore, the rhythm
the tension, the dart and slide
of lives unseen

where water becomes sky
mirrors course-ways of light
like sleep's strange rearrangement
of days when carried in ways

essential and unknown —
slime and muscled silvers
the geo-logic outlying
granite faces

the call and shriek of gulls
motors and horns
the way the surface breaks
the edges in constant motion

like in a mind
every collision and erosion
churning down to sand —
like us, like stones
with the waves inside.

Aqua Sienna

∧

Beneath the plane in the aqua fields
waves of white vapor.
There, a current
steep waterfall of clouds
over an invisible precipice.

∧

Beneath the willow, l lay
my cheek on the shoulder of the river,
a cleft in the body of the earth.
It shines back to the sun, the river
through blades of grass and stones
from a white crest into mist through the fingers
and legs whispering now, now, now
pulling a dark stream.
Red roots stretch from the bank, listening.
Knots are tying, tangles unfurling
boulders shifting.

∧

Underground the rivers
are veins we press upon.
No way to know what they join
or leave or conceive
what stones they ride
or what body they become.

Breaking

Invisible guests come down the road.
The spruce in the last drift throws off its shadow
as darkness looms.
The indirection of wind fills the room
spider webs stretch.
Outside, frost and snow travel like snakes
over the cold streets.
We surround ourselves with digital fields
and sink. Subzero's in the cycle
the dragline to climb.
We backtrack and go forward, untested,
on a ledge suspended over waves
clashing like armies under our feet.
Our weight on that
ice, a mirror covered with steam.

Horses
for Symphony no.2 by Jean Sibelius

∧
In the orchestra, the conductor lifts his arm
reeds and muscles trade

with trembling strings.
The earth tilts a fraction of a degree.

Cymbals are struck, the sound un-leveling.
Horses gallop on distant pastures.

Hollows fill with water. The musicians sweat.
Flashes of silver and black. Burnished brass.

An ear for repercussions. The heartbeat of hooves.
Pearl moon on hot leather.

This body cannot contain its liberations,
nor the fire its sparks.

∧
Before the interment, we set the horses free.
They crossed the empty field
through shadow and made a path to the burial.

They gathered behind us.
The ground split with the weight of a man
and water filled the hollow.

I felt the shovel in my chest.
We placed the young man's ashes, placed fallen feathers
into the underground river,

left notes. Words were taken, the soul
began to travel. The horses
retreated as if the last gate closed in their faces.

The weight is heavy.
I know the horses will return.
Eventually will go over, break free.

∧

At the funeral feast we push back our chairs.
In the ragged hymn, there's the clang of plates,
a hundred horses, racing.

The body with its headache.
The body of the horse rises with its slopes
and glorious veins, dilating

into a poetry of silence. Of mares.
Meanwhile, a boat founders
in a hurricane beyond rescue.

Cries are heard behind glass.
Heat has risen, and there is need for
what will surely never come.

∧

Horses roll into the capillaries
and follow the conductor
from the concert hall to other listening walls.
Blooded, going forward,

at the pace of heartbeats.
Never for the last time, ice with vodka
and cranberry and lime,
blankets wet and steaming.

∧

A circle of quarter horses with braided manes
on diamonds, they prance
with iron shoes

on roads filled with strife.
On a dark night, a strike.
The sound of collapse:

one great wall and a country on its continent.
An opera in the house
and a crisis in the measures.

The circle runs through graves and their instruments
through Sibelius' latitudes
the hands that held the reins.

∧

In horsepower, the soloist excels,
her fragile body
given over to the red violin.

She's a racehorse. Ears back, ears forward.
In chaos and howling war,
the motion of flanks and haunches.

We can't hear our own voices.
We can't tune it out.
Heedless riders, in the ebb of sound.

Hay in the loft spontaneously combusted.
The staves burnt in a white heat.
When the wind dropped, we fell.
Got up again. Shoulders in.

Erosions

A vowel rises from excavations
where roads end in mine pits and tailings ponds
in the headwaters at the top of the Divide.
I add it to the dark rags for my loom

add rock corings and depths of the great lake
to the warp, old growth and timbers that drift.
I ride rails between hills that are mine dumps,
in the wake of prospectors

and speculators with diamond drills. I thread
the weft with strings of a broken horizon.
Between the breast beam and back beam
in the days followed by afternoons followed by graveyards

amid handles and ratchets and beaters
I throw the shuttle, pound the bar
in perpetual motion
ply the treadles in this place of tool and die.

Erosions and accretions pour from the ridges
through minerals and ores.
I hear the taconite plants spilling their waste
and trains pulling heavy loads.

The water, suspect. The paychecks, scanty.
The ships that come in are not ours.
I always thought pines would stay standing
the sun would set on all our lakes. But that's not the case.

Geology won't keep
as the holes grow more deep.
In streams that fall into and out of my lap
I make rugs to throw on the floor.

Disappearing Earth

Beneath the map, a bolt
of heavy lightning
reached into pre-protozoic time
and threw a vein of iron into
the molten ground before the ice age
— we mine it.
The river winds like threads
around the coordinates.
Railroads stitch across the grid.
Towns that sprung up around the open pits
and roads that were built — move.
The Hull and the Rust and the Mahoning
became one mine
and the neighborhood teetered over the edge.
In Hibbing, a hotel slid off the back of a truck
other houses were lifted by jacks
and traveled south somewhere.
Now the main highway has been called back.
The signature's affixed.
Bulldozers tear up concrete
and shovels take over beneath
alter the three-way divide.
Now we cross over the mine pit on a bridge
built by taxpayers.
The company pulled out an old contract
signed by the state.
Every map becomes obsolete
on this temporary topography called tonnage.

Minntac Brand

At nineteen, I entered the gate
followed the road to the taconite plant
Minntac.

Scraped earth, not a stem of green.
In the pit, giant dump trucks
haul tons of rock to the Crusher.

This goes on to the Fine Crusher
and on.
Laborers in the Agglomerator
breathe black dust.
Big furnaces roll the fines into pellets.

The furnace vents fill with hot pellets
have to be emptied into the buckets
of front end loaders by maintenance laborers
wearing asbestos suits.

White pellets were 1000 degrees Fahrenheit
black were 400 degrees.
Pellets could stick to the skin, burn into the neck.
It was called a Minntac brand.

One day, I saw a front-end loader
roll over the foot of a laborer.
They cut off his boot and
called the ambulance.

Conveyors kept rolling.
Broken were nineteen out of twenty-six bones,
the end of his mining career.

Now, there are signs in many yards.
We support mining.
Mining supports us.

Open pits on the Iron Range
scar the landscape.
Underground abandoned mines
are cordoned off by steel fences.
The Hull-Rust pit is visible from space.

There's no mining
without accidents.
You take it or leave it.

Dialectics
from Hegel and Marx

Water to ice.
A change in the nature of a thing.
To go beyond appearances to reality.
To see with my own eyes, to hear, to think
and speak. A language of becoming.
Change is old, a mole
burrowing underground unseen for a long time
that suddenly emerges into the light.
The ground shifts, the surface turns over.
Never anywhere is there matter without motion.
From stop-motion, the river
lifts cornices of ice.
To reach the future of the past.
A chain of changes.
A trigger. A catalyst. A strike.
Propelled by being held back.
Negation of the negation.
To become what it was not.
Contradiction makes motion possible.
Inseparable are causes and effects.
One thing forms and the opposite reforms.
Progress proceeds through a series of contradictions.
The shattering of the old, *a sudden overturn.*

Vulture

On the ridge of Spirit Mountain,
we entered the vulture's house.

Wind stopped as the black umbrella
of wings snapped shut.

We smelled red cedar, Norway pine,
decaying leaves. Mud on our feet

we followed our need in and out of the closet.
Easy to forget many secrets are kept and profit on death.

There are words for this. Vultures
fly in a kettle and land in a volt.

Some call it a committee.
Some call the election a special kind of greed.

Bare heads and bare necks make it easier to feed.
Here, no carcass of deer.

No volt that day on the slope
nor broken down house ruined by men.

To the mountain, this lone bird came to her nest.
The wake was somewhere else.

At the Edge

In the high wind off democracy
seagulls stopped scavenging
for French fries and crusts of bread.

People on the shore zip their jackets
tuck their hands in their pockets
keep their heads down.

Waves gray as the granite ledge
break the news of more erosions.
The battering continues.

The goal: run a profitable business.
Slices of banks tumble into the motion.
Ice goes traveling along the streets.

Populations are going extinct.
Deaf to the weathermen's predictions
we march to the will of the people

or not, to the president's decrees.
Nobody is having a picnic.
The seagulls know.

They are suspended in the forces
waiting to be fed.
Their wings lifting.

Antenna Farm

Towers on the hill hold rivers
of invisible transmissions.
Day and night, red warning lights
and high frequencies
send voices of lovers, worried parents,
or people who are looking.
Endless robo-calls.
Messages. Megahertz.
Deer come to graze in the fields
but don't stay beneath the bounce
of news, no news.
On their migrations, hawks
on the geo-thermals
don't divert their flights.
One night, at the base of a tower,
a woman died at the hands
of her assailants.
Nobody came to her rescue
but the grass bowed over her body.
The fox hurried along the edge
of the clearing to look in her face.
The crows gathered.
Detectives found no evidence.
No charges were filed.
Static fills the radios
pixels drift over a threshold
as people pick up, don't pick up
in the new language
the one made of zeros and ones.

Losing Ground

From upstairs I watched the endless rain.
The hill washed down the slope.
I saw the river's dark side, sinkholes and mudslides and speed.
Earth and water rose to the bridge.

Three doors down, the foundation of a house buckled
teetered over the edge. Clung to the wires.
Down the hill, the sumps could not pump and
water rose in the basements.

High water scoured the banks, moved boulders, uprooted
lifted old pines into arms of the younger.
Rails of bridges caught tree trunks.
Bridge decks got knocked off the pylons.

Neighbors went out to stare at what was no longer there.
A car was parked. The ground beneath it sunk six feet.
Brewer's Creek, buried years ago, burst
through the macadam and removed the grocery parking lot.

At the zoo, seals washed away. The polar bear
escaped its cage and walked through the alley.
In the cemetery, graves lost their names
and unburied the coffins.

In the west a child swept into a storm drain
came out alive.

Trace

On the thawing ground, I found
a robin's nest,
a coil of mud and dry grass
woven around a single chamber.

I've worked like this
for the same result
something of my own disappearing.

My own child, grown and flown.
My old houses, abandoned,
the love sputtered out.

Every year, I enter the forest
and pick up broken shells
or the skull of a deer.
And now this, a drab and hollow nest.

When the robins return, they will build
a new work of art
only to be discarded again.
They will march across the yard and guard

that space. Will sing.
I must put it on my sill, to remember
in next year's unfamiliar spring:
how empty is the natal place.

Broken Shell

Before the earth, in the *Kalevala*,
a virgin of the air Ilmatar
wandered the high altitudes
with time on her hands.

The ocean lured her in.
She slapped the water, flirted
with wind and the wind dared
or the waves slid along her thighs
quickened in her empty womb —

she swam seven hundred years
with salt upon her tongue.
In solitude. A child within.

She heard a lonesome note in the sky,
some winged thing
searching for a land to build a nest.
In reply, lifted her knee, an island.
The hen came to nest
laid seven eggs. One was iron.

The hen set to brooding.
The nest so hot
Ilmatar in the indigo deep
couldn't keep still
twitched like an earthquake
and the eggs all broke.

One half shell formed dry earth
Terra, and the other half
the aqua vault.
One yolk became sun
and albumen, clouds
and the Milky Way.

The litter of shells
veins of iron and copper.
Ilmatar moved clay
beneath her feet to make reefs
and deeps for a silver cloud of herring
and icebergs calving.

Made the headlands
and mountains to hold up the sky
Unfolded the continents
drew out the rivers.

This is how Ilmatar's labor began.
Exertion became a waterfall.
From her moon's chamber
through the bony gate
she gave birth to a singer,
an earth diver.

Named him Väinämöinen.
Already he was an old man.

∧

Winds rippled through grain fields
and swayed the dense forests.

The singer plucked at strands
on the jawbone of a fish,
hän lauloi laulun.
Laulaa taivanrannalle,
to sing to the sky's beach.

Loud migrations darkened the sky.

In the waves were multitudes.

Canadian Geese
in memory of Floyd

Radio signals wandered. The road a dark avenue north
through Seven Mile Swamp and the crossings of deer.
Our union went by land and water, under the stars, our truck
pulling a boat and motor in a blizzard of moths.

To live by the mine and not mine. To store, not excavate.
In the winter, to hunt rabbits and partridge,
leap and burst and flight.
To climb into the stand for the annual buck.
See how the body smooths the rough bark of the tree.

To hunt moose. Gut and quarter the body. Fry moose liver
in a cast iron pan, in onions. Sew a jacket from its hide
on a shoemaker's treadle machine. Trim the hood
with wolfskin and line it with goose down.

To form a small country, population two.
Carry water. Between killing frosts, plant flats of tomatoes
and can rows of red innards, tomato hearts
in wide-mouthed jars. Rows of deer meat, in gravy,
sealed in a pressure cooker.

To pick berries. Chop wood. Ignore the years between us.
In the spring opener, accustom ourselves to the rocking
of the boat in wave after wave. To anchor in the cold,
holding lines. At New Year's, turn a hand auger
and make a hole in the ice.

To jig for lake trout in a polar vortex,
the day bright with sundogs. Camp on the ice.
Warm our tent with a stove. Bale water from the floor.
To sleep at forty below zero. Hear the lake making ice,
a sound like thunder, except from beneath.

To find our melting point. Our boiling point.
To smoke trout. Wrap in butcher paper.
Set a table with the prize fish
served with cream cheese and slices of cucumber.
Drink vodka. Heat the pie
in the wood stove and eat.

Anything could be fixed, a propeller caught in the weeds,
the boat grounded on a reef or a broken leg.
Staples worked themselves through the skin after many years.
He moved the course of a small river. A forest was making
and unmaking.

We measured the old pines, built a house and dock
in another country. Made a child.
I can't own this, not even the words.
In May, my mother tied a scarf at her nape
and played a game of chance. Didn't win.

Life runs on whim and temper.
On this red morning, through sweeping balsam
comes the deer to the bird feeder.
The sunflowers grew fast and spent their seeds.
Our stake melted like snow. We thought it would last,
but Canadian geese contradicted us flying overhead.

In the Mind of the Forest

Balsams tapped my sleeves as I tramped into corridors
through the mind of the forest that owns me.
In its gaze, the trunks were not trunks but masts.

They were beams of an infinite pavilion with a floor
not level but built on the slopes and troughs of a wave.
The snow was not blue as the sky, but sifted, drifted

from that hue, not blue as the lake but lifted like vapor.
Or as from stars, although misted and dusted.
In the machinery of wind in the rolling cloud of forest

I could feel the land lift and drop.
A branch broke its tip, scented me with pitch.
I put my weight on a city of fungus.

In the clearing, close to the frozen cataract of the pond
gray as wasps' nests among the vertical lines
wolves spoke from their shoreless territories

a song of lament and rejoicing. Things repeat, rhyme,
underline. Words spoken aloud have a vibration that travels
around the earth in the wind overhead.

I went past tree stumps sharpened like spears near
the ice-latched beaver lodge and its exhalations
through fallen rooms of light.

Under the layers of years, there was once a farm here
a cultivated field. There were children, arguments,
and convictions replaced by seedlings that turned into trees

and trees kept propagating even among the dead.
I met those without roots, those that levitate,
those that break as much as bend and hang on nothing.

I heard the bark of trees being printed and bound,
saw the mark of claws on a trunk and piercing by beaks.
In the eaves of spruce trees

crows hung their capes. A Medusa reared, roots
pulled up by counterweight. From the ground
a boulder crested. Above, an owl sat motionless, seeing

all that was hidden and nameless.
I passed an open grave ribboned by shade
and stepped through the vapor of sleep into a wild bed.

Strange Beasts: Boulder Lake

Wind tears through aspens
scatters yellow leaves upon the waves
raises conflicting territories

turns and counterturns
against the shoulders of Moose Island.
I paddle away from the dam

over clumps of seaweed
over cutover and vestiges of old growth
in water tinted by tannins.

A lone eagle circles high over Lady Island.
Rising levels had joined Little Boulder and Boulder
Lake with Otter Lake.

The massive boulders grow moss
on their backs, fine blades of grass
ripple in the wind like fur.

Roots of the white pines have drowned
and their trunks rotted. In cauldrons of gray stumps
water swirls in the basins.

On the banks, driftwood lies like beasts
gone extinct in midstride and petrified.
Near Wolf Bay, the elephant stone draws close.

The most temporary am I. Like fog
drifting. Small islands
and large stones seem to glide.

On the surface of the water, wild rice
lays itself down
and my boat slides over its blades.

We sway in the waves.
Four otters surface and hiss
Four otters like waterspouts.

Way Finding

To cross the wilderness is to lose all bearings
make too many tracks mostly in the wrong direction.
To know the halves of it, the creation and destruction.
To follow an azimuth and advance by degrees
toward a zenith, the method used by munitions.
Maybe the core is meant to be on a frictionless pivot.
No way to calibrate the gap between geographical
and magnetic North. To not call this lost.
Not call this found.

Snail

As the river rises, I carry my own house.

In a labyrinth of vertical dimension, climb
into a new tongue,

push blindly on, even as the riverbank collapses
even when plucked by a bird and dropped into a port.

I scale the docks, trace seaweed for diatoms,
open the lids and dine in the bins.

I follow my own method
harden the shell to protect myself

look toward space
emissions and reflections dark and planetary

as if nebulae were my map or the swirl
of falling water.

Blue

    Trempeleau, Wisconsin

The earth below the blue October sky
belongs to herons, rails, terns, pelicans, and egrets.

Blue hills belong to the Mississippi,
the thousand mallards, blue-winged teal and wood ducks
feeding in the blue shallows.

The mud flats belong to the cattails, bur reed,
sedges, bulrush. The bottom land to the silver maple,
river birch, swamp white oak, cottonwood, willow, and ash.

The algae on the water to the after-rain
where the prairie meets river bottom
to the sky where lines of pelicans turn south.
White feathers tipped with black.

Currents above, around, and beyond.
Moonlight looking after moonlight.
All hollow bones.
All words departed. Every heartbeat taken wing.

The Otherworld

Vene / Boat

I sent my green boat across the border
over waves past the island of birch.

Into the mouth of the River of Pohjola
with hard rapids, standing edges of swords.
Half in, half out.

The bow slams waves that hit back
and break over the sides
filling the hold with their weight.

The boat goes over heartbreak
where a wall has fallen.
Under the water an old record spins

into an underwater forest.
My green boat,
shuddering, plunging sideways

through clouds and water.
An axe converses
with stones, converses with water.

I glide on momentum overtaken by wake
into a bay where the waters lay.
The loon has built her nest behind a rock.

The small ones follow their mother
as she calls, wild music.
Laughing, as if the world were new.

Kieli / Tongue

Speak in the other language
where none of the vowels drown.
They roll on the tongue in motion.
Speak in shades of brown
in sky and wind
in water spilling.

Speak with river's logic
with velocity or amplitude
in rifts and riffles
reaching and unraveling.
Otherwise, meandering.
Otherwise, standing.
Beneath the surface
a fast current departing.

Speak through mud and roots
with no premise other than a stone
no conclusion
other than a channel
to cut the bank, to shear
fall over and between.

Although the river questions,
it drops, deepens,
finds an opening, an emphasis.
A season.

Satama / Harbor

On the wet sand of the Baltic
small wavelets and beyond, swells rise
not my grandmother's life
which has landed
on another continent, but mine
embarking
from maybe or between.

Kalevala Viidestoista Runo / Poem 15

for Akseli Gallen-Kallela's *Lemminkäinen Äiti* painting

The signs of his blood have led
to the banks of the Tuonela River.
I kneel on red stones,
on skulls and broken bones.

A swan, distant witness,
draws in a circle of silence.
My eyes see what is underneath
in the rapids of death, my son.

I rake his bones
his scattered parts
take them back from the spirits,
back from the bottom.

I rub the ointments into his joints.
Seal the wounds
using glue that will never let go.
I push, make new contractions in his muscles.

I bend low, unburying memory
and sing for I have found him
breathless. I sing to the tiny stones
rolling beneath our weight

I sing the swan's notes.
New lines come. Lungs toss up
runnels of the river through his nose.
Minnows swim from his throat.

I take him back not into my body
that conceived, received, and raised this one
but back to his own. To the sun.
Darkness watches, his eyes like stones.

With a needle, I pierce the broken ends
and pull my thread.
I turn the edges, commend to God.
Say, remember him.

Take this cold back to the reaching ice
seize this body with new breath.
I shake the heart to make it start ticking
as I drop it into place

put back the ribs and pull up the skin.
On the stones, he gasps.
Where I have wept and pounded.
On the shore where I have assembled him.

Rannalla / On the Beach

After the cities
with their sharp horns and teeth,
I find a place on the beach

under the deep blue dome, empty,
filled with light and vapor.

Somebody has built a structure that barely stands.
I perch on the bleached bones of a tree
too wet to burn, silver like me.

Behind is a cut bank.
On the horizon, two ships wait as the sun heats.

The wind bends the waves.
Lavender no longer breaks on the sand
but slides into sepia.

Red sand fills the hollows.
A woman walks along the edge.

Children run into the currents and out.
Chains of the boats pull at the anchors.
There is so much weight.

Soon I will be full of sand
soon I'll drift.

I can hear the whisper of blades
in dune grass: come closer — don't come.

Kääntää / To Translate

On the dock, an old woman
lowers herself into the dark Baltic
swims with long strokes past the orange floats,
unmistakable channel markings.

I search for words, for conveyance.
The tongue with an old root.
Kääntää means to translate.
Kantaa means to carry.

I swim with her, let her arms
pull me to and from
the pine forest, *suomen mäntymetsä*.
the real and wavering image.

The sun is sinking
as she emerges, takes off her swimming cap
pulls herself up on the land as she
shakes off the water.

If only there were a word for this
Ilmatar forming the body of earth.
If memory was gold, a fly caught in amber.

Katsoa / To Look

In the morning sun translates blades of grass
back from the ice.

Sheep rise from sleep to investigate my route.
They are long-haired, brown and white.

The long road turns to mud. Fields slope to a still lake.
Three swans swim and pull behind a single wake.

There, a coarse cry. Was this the sound I heard
as a girl the morning when my grandmother died?

Or was this the sound of birth?
The sound of the sun as it rises from the reeds?

Looking into yards, I find a woman raking leaves
chasing leaves, finding only more leaves.

Hämähäkki / Spider

A spider works in this slant of sunlight —
in long shadows
like grandmother with her spools making lace
out of holes, out of knots.

It's all I have, that edging
she made for the pillow where I sleep.
I remember her dark hair with silver threads
the heavy brows.

The spider travels from the center
to a high corner I could never reach.

In silence, in gaps we speak in the old language
inch along narrow threads
work in drafts
rearrange the alphabet in loops and lines.

Her fingers moved the bobbins back and forth.
Even shoes at the door have eyes, a tongue.

She untied and fastened somewhere else.

I look for her words
watch a spider anchor and glide.
Some threads wrap. Some lead.

Roukaa / Food

In every aisle
in the ruokatavarat
grocery store —
leipää, juustoa, munat, kahvia
bread, cheese, eggs, coffee,
grandmother's words come to my hands.
Things salty and sweet,
sour and creamy.
Now with the items in the cart
I roll to the till with a child's language,
so they can ring this up
and I can pay any price.
Voi mummon kieltä, älä unohda minua.
Oh grandmother's tongue, do not forget me.

Lautasen / Plates

Planks of the dock rocked with my footsteps

November's lake trembled. Tall cattails, bleached by cold,
some bent.

Broad leaves of seaweed drifted like empty plates.
A minnow was served to bigger fish.

Today I went to the graves lost in the mist.
On these flat stones black and polished, my names.

After her death, my grandmother's china joined the diaspora.
Nevertheless, once I found a plate
just like hers in a second-hand store
and brought it home for my kitchen cupboard.

Pulled by the currents of wind
at the cemetery, I closed the gate.

Maybe I should say something else.
The minnow was chosen.

Hevonen / Horse

At a crossing in the rain. On clay ground at a Y.
On one side were cultivated fields.
On the other an entire forest in moss a foot deep.
There I could see a mother stone.

I could see a horse farm like my home
and watch a woman throw hay over the fence.
I could have been her sister.

I might have planted these furrows
gathered chanterelles and lingonberries.

I turned back where these brown horses
tore at bales of hay and seasons passed.
The summer — one long day
and winter — one long night.

Once I rode a dump rake behind my father's tractor
rode on a horse that moved like a wave on the sea
picked white flowers in May.

I once touched the soft muzzle.
My hand stroked the crest and withers
I heard the rub of reins, the jingle of a halter
the groan of the saddle.

Smelled the dusty wool saddle blanket,
the horse's flanks and mane and tail.

Sammal / Moss

From the road, I noticed
a green shaggy bear.
Coming closer, it turned into windfall
from a storm,
a wheel of roots pulled from the ground
propped next to a fallen trunk,
both grown over and thick with moss
that grows on the living and the dead,
takes everything back to silence.

I was deep in that silence
when I noticed a spruce tree
with a broken top,
resembling a headless giant, a woman,
a pillar of the earth.
Boughs were arranged like a skirt
on her long torso.
Full of wind's motion, striding.

Mitä Jos Sota / What If a War

In the night I heard a voice crying or laughing.
In Finland. I had just arrived —
pulled up the window blind
on heavy rain and saw a beam of light
that stroked the wind-lashed tree.

The person holding the flashlight, unseen,
speaking in the other language.
I picked up my phone to see
3:03 a.m. and a news alert.
Terrorists attacked Bataclan in Paris.

That day, I remembered seeing
a long line of military vehicles, dark green
with camouflage over their loads
going through town. Assumed this was routine.
Remembered my mother Siiri.

She prized the one-way ticket
to the new country.
If I even mentioned a desire to see
where my grandparents were born,
she became frantic, as if under siege.

What if a war breaks out?
If you can't get back? Then what?
Civil strife, the Winter War,
World War I and II,
the Russian interventions in Eastern Europe.
Her evidence.

Thirty years later — I listen
to what I don't understand.
How long it had taken me to come!

Kuppi Jäkälä / Cup Lichen

for Helvi Juvonen

In the palaces of wilderness,
come to a small table.
Bird wings, above the open crowns of pines
in motion.
Below, wind only a breath
easy to mistake for your own.
Near are hidden movements of deer
or if not there,
then wolf and moose, or rabbit and lynx
the unlimited and narrow paths —
long streams in a boreal ocean.
Their lives are secret
and you in their lair. Listen with your eyes.
Sunlight comes between shadows.
Lingonberries drop down a digestive tract.
Here on the moss, *sammal*,
everything diminishes. Mushrooms.
Kanttarellit.
For every death
waits a kingdom of insects
and cups filled with rain.

Talvi / Winter

My hands gripped the steering wheel in the blizzard.
Not driving but falling through the night,

in the shine of headlights, tiny meteors or stars,
going to the center.

Upward, I was taken.
Behind, all tracks disappearing.

Illumination from below:
snow becomes clouds, and clouds become drifts.

Ahead, unfurled, a fresh canvas
and trees writing themselves into dark ink.

Sunnuntai / Sunday

Let me be in the lichen
in the leaf-shorn birch
in the dark spruce
and red stems of sphagnum
inside the rain and mist in half light.

Let me be in the breath of the lake
layered by vowels in the fields
between furrowed sleep and spring seed
in cloud's light.

Let me be far
in the wind in the whisper
of the wood fire
in the heat, in the arms
of long-lit stars
on the wings of the aurora.

Revontulet / Aurora Borealis

Stars shake off swaths of dust and fire.

I too disrobe under the small roof
of the sauna. There is a girl here, a mother
and grandmother.

Inside the mirror, silver and white
clouds and shadow and heat.
Inside the stove, an orange conflagration
compressing and spending.

Wood smoke drifts into the blue.
Rocks hiss. Birch leaves slap and sweeten the skin.
I am here
inside my grandmother's body. In the dark fields

grooves of the plow wait
for the snow's light, for spring's seed.

I shake the towels.
Sky's sheets unfurl.

Kengät / Shoes

Hämeenkyrö, Finland

At Runoklubi, I accidentally photographed
my brown shoes under the table.

On stage, the poet performed in blue shoes
with a raspberry and white wave
on the edge of each of his soles.

Applauding —
I could never wear shoes like that
but then, I can hardly wear any.

Other people have smart ankle boots
tight-fitting, sleek, flexible.
On this trip, I brought just one pair, a mistake.

My feet are hot, they need to change a lot,
require air. They ache. The arches need stroking.
My heels want to go.

My feet swell. Maybe I need
adjustments in
Attitude. Size. Speed.

These shoes are one-way only.
I must buy another pair
for the trip back home.

Headwaters

Identity

The grasses stitch but don't hold me.

I am taken by gravity
fill containers perfectly
yet my shores are ever wandering.

I quench and am never quenched
shift from state to state,
invisible through impenetrable.

Throw in one stone.
I draw myself in circles concentrically.
Linguistically.

The body acts out versions and
submersions and immersions

echoes that echo, reverse
and have an undertow.
The body compensates —
falls, rises, condensates.

Current

> *Every word is either current or strange*
> —Aristotle

I travel for the constant unraveling
that deprives me of words
to start over again with strange letters

to amend the old grammar
to seek arrangements from disarrangement
to seep, to spill, to pour.

Without an itinerary, I raid
the past and run over banks
abandon my accretions

to fall into a new mouth.

Pussywillows

because we used to have roots
but now wander along roads anonymous
rise from the last traces of snow
covered with dust and dirt

because when the sun bends down
with arms of light
we reach up, aching and tired,
knowing she would find us

because we like to hide
these thin brittle arms
with gray and silver buds
that bring no scent of mud or spring
no blossom or color

because it's a newborn touch
filled with memories of rabbit fur
when your mother snipped branches
and arranged them in a jar
on the table for the feast

because we are long gone and here
and part of that circle
that must be found every year
to bring this gift

No Other Morning like This

I waited a long time for daybreak
listening to the faint sound of a battery in the clock
each minute measured, mechanical
slowly pushing away from my father's last breath.
There is never a line you can see
between night and morning — they come out of each other.

I turned the alarm off before it rang.
The day to make arrangements.
The first day in the world without him, ever again
and in the wan light, my feet found the floor.
Toward the sound of coffee, voices,
I groped my way back that long hallway.

Weight
Knife River Beach

In heat and smoke,
I watch the blue fire of Lake Superior
the way water burns into light
the island where the gulls bask and lift
the long-distance wind carrying their cries.

Children on the beach
call cold-cold
submerge to their knees, fold their arms
like landing birds.
Drought rattles the leaves.

The children laugh and scream in delight
dive like ducks
as clouds thicken
over the wildfire.

The shore's edge is restless
defies prediction
overestimates, falls short and then gains.
A billion years, these stones rolled.
Farther north, ash falls like snow.

Weight falls under the surface
of the lake where gods
haul the deep swells. Teams of workhorses
harness to this rolling weight
don't break at the task
bring in all they can carry.

Names

To say earth — the blue voice
of Lake Superior
speaks to the ledge of rock.
To say pine — an eagle lifts
from the tall crown of the Norway.

Into the circle of given and taken
naming goes on.
In every language, this is the work
never done.
There is no last word.
They lie down together, entwine.

To say horses, they graze
in the mist.
As they pull the grass
their tails swish away deer flies.

To say woman —
there's beginning without end.
To say children — there's the tight bud.
To say man — seeds take root,
a construction of strong deeds.

To speak is to mend.

The Dark Season

I walk in the field
and cast seeds into the furrows,
let go of all my holdings.

Impossible to predict which blossoms will turn to fruit.
Impossible to tell what intricacy will unfold.

Impossible not to travel into winter and cold
not to meet anger or complacency.
I open my palm
release to the wind
my needs and apprehensions.

I don't mind volunteers from other places
weeds or opportunities.

My aim is not to deliberate
only to abandon the little things,
knowing for root and stem to grow
the split must come.

West Two Rivers

Summer on the river in Zim
beneath the bridge.
Three girls swam in the currents.
We left our towels
on the steep bank in the long grass.
The water, dark as amber
or tea. It was cold. Spring fed.
We could cross from one side
to the other. We could
step in the drop-off, not drown.
Cows grazing upon the ridge
kept an eye on us.
Then a bell rang and they went
across the field into the barn
which used to be the Woullet house.
The cows were in the old kitchen.
We never knew the Woullets —
didn't know the past at all
although it cast us out of its door.
Now hooves scraped
floors once washed clean.
Manure was piled high
outside the door
beside yellow dandelions.
The cows chewed their cud
and looked out the windows
at the evening light,
while my uncle tied their tails
with binder twine before milking.
We salted our toes

to make the blood-suckers let go.
We put our shoes back on wet feet
to walk over the new mown hay.
We climbed over the log gate
and ran toward a new house.
I've come to know that freedom now.
It winds across the landscape
calling like girls' voices.

St. Louis River Route

The river unraveled like a yarn
through the forest.
I paddled the canoe
held the arms of wind-fallen
trees and pulled the boat
through the shallows.
I walked on the bottom
of the river, in its light,
went over the path
of the French explorer
who renamed
the river after another king
over the trail
of floating bunk houses
and cook shacks
when there were log drives.
I paddled past immigrants,
my Finnish grandparents,
past beaver traps and hoop nets
past wood ducks and mallards,
over the catfish,
walleyes, northern pike
and smallmouth bass.
Paddled past moose
and bears and timber wolves,
past white-tailed deer and ruffed grouse.
Under the pines
I was going nowhere in particular
was going to stop
was staying afloat, getting here.

At the Threshold

Sandpipers race along the edge
waves arrive with driftwood and depart,
taking sand from the beach.

Freighters come empty and leave
with the earth.

A feather comes and I catch it
on my way to the dunes.
Things that are lost are more than ever the things I carry.

Those that have passed walk with me.
Only by leaving did they arrive
to talk of things that we never could have spoken.

I slept and dreamed of being awake.
But when I awoke, went about in dreams,
emptied when I might have filled.
Laughed when I might have cried.

A wind presses against the house,
and goes, taking the house away.

Departure
Kakagi Lake, Ontario, 2019

The dock upon the night waters
led to a violet sky.
We went in the gray fishing boat and motor
on the old route, my son and I.

I did not think I'd return this way
after thirty years.
I was a sapling and now an old willow.
What was once a field of dandelions
is now a dark forest.

A ghost shadowed my steps. I saw him in my son
who went to swim and catch fish.
I saw him in the woodstove where a fallen bird
had burned, trying to fly.

I found large stones and a granite face.
Pine trees grown fifty feet.
Cedars thick and green. I did not sleep.
Footings had sunk.
The stream had fallen undergound.

A story I'd started had been taken over by others.
Reading their words
helped me see past my own death.
What seemed immovable was shifting.
Stacks of boards. Fishing tackle on the tables.
Ceaseless accumulation.

Lucky, I say, to cross over
and see new grandchildren on the slope.
To smell sun in their hair.
To give this all away.

The water lapped on shore
and loons called in the night.
A bear walked by unseen but left its mark.

Map / The Way Back
for Rai 1988–2017

Take the old road into the north.
Turn left and right past the Big Noise
over mud and frost boils to the old place
past logging trucks and gravel pits
past steam shovels
and horses galloping back and forth.

Remember the old growth
before the excavations,
the rivers before iron and taconite,
the skies over the Divide.
Remember the spark and flame,
the fire in the forge,
the iron in the earth
before it became steel,
the circles before the wheel.

Go through farms and cow pastures
past cars and their parts,
over rocks and through gates.
Travel the chain of lakes
with no beginnings or ends
portage around beaver dams
swim when you must
north around the bends
through cattails
past pine and broken birch
under tangle and windfall.

Take the song back into the bird's heart.
Sway the way your mother once swayed
holding you in her arms.
Under the glint of stars
where clouds gather and break.
Follow the roots of the white pine
back through soft needles
back to the cone. Unseal.
Let the birds take those seeds.

Half-Fallen One

In the forest, a slash.
Hard limbs hold a half-fallen tree
interrupted between ascent and descent.

I could not determine the condition of its roots
or the cause of its demise
whether by beetles or the force of wind.
I could not guess what weight or sway
might bring it down.

Underneath are footprints of rabbit and wolf.
Squirrels climb and birds alight.
Obstacle or miracle,
between gravity and flight.

Luck

When we registered at the hotel
paid for the room
the clerk dropped change in our palms
and we split the Sacajawea coins.
Two women, two dollars each.
Liberty was emblazoned over her head
and on her left shoulder In God We Trust
and on the flipside, an eagle flying.
The coins clicked in our pockets
as we opened the door of our room.
It was fortuitous, this goddess
bringing us through the wilderness
to that room where
daylight fell on the mountains and valleys
of the sheets
and the soundtrack played A Case of You.
It was a cold March
and we were behind glass
looking out to Lake Superior
steam rising from the hot tub.
We fed each other slices of oranges
and focaccia pierced by
small arrows of rosemary.
The flying-by clouds propelled the wind
that circled the earth and came back again.
We were in a river that could not stop.
I rubbed the coins for luck
and the woman whose face I touched
led us onward,
explorers of the light,

not taking land
not trading in counterfeits.
We came up for breath on the river delta.
This was not luck but legal tender.
Sacajawea crossed our palms
and her eagle flew from the past
into the morning. We dove in.

Yoni

On a cold not so cold
morning
with clouds overhead
I came to your bed.
On the foot bridge
I looked down into the crevice
in the ice.
It was February
and night's river flowing
from underground
and back again.
The sound,
an earthy invitation.
A cervix of water
widening
in the throes of labor
the river about to
crown, brown again.

Underwater Music

Water is not my instrument
although we play it.

Without holding a beat
it plays back, goes without settling.

In the body that holds your body
where forces alter gravity
the sound is falling. Waves
roll down in currents
of C notes and unplayed keys
sliding and chords bumping.

This is a heavy going
a soaking, a slowing.
Nothing adds up, all the
evaporating condensing
raining into.

The feet are not on the ground
but they're dancing.

Spring

The river roars.
Rains press on the leaves
of the cherry tree.
Rain's fingers play the ivory
rims of the blossoms
and open the bottom of their bowls.
Near and far the robins bring
weavings to their nests.
Wings brush wings at close range.
The levers of wind, the plunging roots,
the rain down the stem of each leaf
through intersections
down trunks
striations into streams.
Rain saturates the route of bees.
My grief, unburying.
No other music falls this way,
from clouds through full blossoms.

A Ghazal: Without Sinking
for Hildur Guðnadóttir

Fog ascends and descends on broken ladders
in sun's fire. Under the surface, collapsing architectures.

A sunken ribcage. Bubbles from the deep.
In the uncharted cave, twisting and glacial corridors

inhabited by shadows. Unknown spawnings,
suspensions and ripples of predators.

Below the horizon. On the surface, laughter.
On the surface, tension. A slow churn of trawlers.

Fire in the distance. Sparks rise
and the clouds climb and dive like otters.

In the place between chords, afloat.
Four strings of the cello, drifting registers.

The decrescendo of the dock and anchors
the sway of the crib and its timbres.

Flashes of lightning horizontal and vertical.
Bluebottles water-logged. The visible arterial.

An aquasphere of planes, volumes, parallel lines,
rhythms through dark matter.

Ode to Where
for Kathy

In the forest, where the river breaks free
we sleep in the resonant room back-to-back
close to the cello that sways on the night sea,
an ancient boat whose chamber empties perpetually.

Your hand trembles on the bedsheet in sleep
the thick callouses and grooves on the fingertips
remember each quicksilver string. The force you have
to plunge your bow into the invisible

and drive an arrow of notes in the air.
How not known, never known, the instrument's dreams.
The tumble into the great falls, the rush of the body
over the edge on the jagged earth

so deep. We resurface and look for each other
reach for – a breath, a handhold
the unwritten score etched on each of your palms
where forces circle and improvise.

The moon shines on its shelf and the river goes
and cello composes its grief
on parallel wires bound by night hours
rising in upward flights.

Dawn

I woke to an acre of mayflies
a lace of water lilies and weeds
before and after
nudges of waves
coming to and from the island
a cloud on the water, thick pollen afloat
and lines crossing.
Having slept beneath stars
I overestimated depths
and underestimated distances.
Underwater, a flash
of brown and silver walleyes.
The shore's edge a mix of tenses
and mosquitoes chased by dragonflies.
Ducks swim over the wakes
of loons' landings. Time's
concentric circles widen,
the forgotten, the remembered
and forsaken.
Over my head, the slow flap of a heron
a flock of starlings.

Coda

Displacements

I was born into two languages, born of two families who came from western Finland across the Baltic and Atlantic to settle in Minnesota. My grandparents' language, my parents' first language, became waves. Their words sank beneath the surface as I entered my adult life, but the music of their language rose in me.

Finnish requires a different placement of the tongue and a different way to hold the mouth. In Finnish the word for lake is *järvi*. The j is pronounced as y in English. The ä indicates a short vowel sound, like in the word hand. An r is always rolled. The i is pronounced as a long e. The Finnish language is imagistic and close to nature. *Taivaanranta*, for instance, translates to *sky's beach*. The Finnish language uses noun endings instead of prepositional phrases. For example, the Finnish word *vene* which means *boat* undergoes numerous transformations which might mean going to the boat, coming from it, being inside the boat or being outside of it. The suffix, the end of the word, conveys necessary information. In a sentence, Finnish words undergo systematic consonant changes, vowel harmonies, harmonic suffixes and rhythms that reach a dimension of melody. This music rolled like a river through my childhood.

∧

Northern Minnesota has many lakes and rivers. As we were bringing the boats to paddle on Stewart Lake, a helicopter lifted a red bucket over the trees and went north, carrying water to the Greenwood wildfire, burning through 40 square miles. Beyond, in the Boundary Waters, were two more fires, the John Ek fire and Whelp Fire. The air was hazy with smoke. On the water, I was in my blue kayak and my paddling partner in her red one. We approached our landmark rock. Because of the low water levels, the boulder sat much higher above the surface than usual, just like the islands. The wind was intense. We went along the east side and then returned to shore as another helicopter with a red bucket flew north. I see it now as if from a distance. The red bucket under the helicopter had the orb shape of an eye, and it was swaying with sloshing water. As I looked, the image seemed to expand and contract, the way things magnify and shrink underwater.

Home from kayaking later that day, I noticed a black spot in the upper corner of my vision in my left eye. In brightly lit rooms, it was hardly noticeable. When I walked into a darkened room, the spot flipped over like a tadpole. I noticed more floaters, a long black fiber that was like a bit of grass or spider's web located between my eye and the objects that I could see, revealing a third dimension that I had not realized existed.

Two days later, the doctor who examined my vision diagnosed a posterior vitreous detachment. The vitreous, which starts out being like jello when one is young, thins out with age. What I was seeing, he explained, is called flashing. It is caused by the vitreous tugging on the retina. He added that the floaters might move to the center of my vision. You'll get used to it, he assured. The brain adjusts and you won't notice anymore. He went on talking about the anatomy of the eye, but I was thinking one of those floaters looked like a taconite fiber.

∧

When one buys a blue boat, it seems one sees a lot of blue boats. This could be a law about synchronicity in the universe or this could be that noticing is a habit of the mind. A friend observed something about this manuscript: it's underwater. Not only under but over and through. It's about water and volume displacing other volumes.

These poems travel through migration, mining excavations and waterways vulnerable to environmental damage and climate change in Minnesota, where the Northern Continental Divide crosses the Laurentian Divide and creates three watersheds that flow into the Mississippi River, the Great Lakes, and Hudson Bay. These are stories and images, historical and contemporary, about people who are displaced, whose languages are replaced by another language, and who find a fluid space full of gaps, silence, and risk. The book has gone through numerous changes, and it has even turned over, like lakes turn over. The bottom has risen to the top and the surface has sunk.

A manuscript in progress stays fluid for a long time. This project began while I was at Arteles, an artists' retreat in Hameenkyrö, Finland. Besides my grandparents, I thought of current immigrants. I thought of the many people who are displaced by climate change and violence. Immigrants navigate huge changes in landscape, language, and culture. Often, they overcome these barriers without many or any resources. The Ellis Island National Museum of Immigration near the Statute of Liberty displays old posters expressing the resentments against immigrants. Although points of origin have changed, attitudes have not. Because of fear of this judgment, my mother tried to extinguish her Finnish accent.

The book is also about other surface displacements, the mining excavations in my landscape. The Mesabi Iron Range is an area

3 miles wide and 120 miles long, a water-rich landscape and an industrial one. According to the Minnesota Department of Natural Resources, 4.1 billion tons of ore and taconite have been shipped away. Already mining has permanently altered the three-way divide and the path of flowing water.

Thomas F. Waters, author of *The Free-Flowing River*, says rivers are erosional landscapes. As a river flows forward in a valley and carves itself deeper, the valley travels backward. As a river flows forward, its waterfalls move backward. It isn't just the edges or banks of the river that erode, but also the river bottom. There are forces in the landscape that pull in opposite directions, much like forces in our culture.

∧

First, tribal nations inhabited the region of what is now Minnesota. Lake Esquagama, where I grew up, was an important location early in history. According to historian Marvin Lamppa, the burial mounds around Esquagama, which date back to the year 1000 A.D., were made by the Woodland Indians. Not much is known about their culture. Near the mounds, arrowheads have been found and copper implements made from the copper deposits in the area. Other tribes came after the Woodland people. As the United States population grew and settlers and immigrants moved westward, the eastern tribes were pushed west as well. The Anishinaabe people came to Minnesota in the mid-1800s, and with them, the vision of food that grows on water, Manoomin or wild rice. The Iron Range is where my grandparents arrived in the early 1900s, along with hundreds of thousands of other immigrants. When they came, over forty languages were spoken on the Iron Range. No other region was as diverse except for New York City.

The past is underwater somehow, sunken and like Atlantis. Maybe the past lacks oxygen, but I have been diving into the wreck, as Adrienne Rich said in her famous poem. I have been inspired by Meridel Le Sueur's words, "Let yourself down, as if underwater, into these lost walls, to hunt for treasure, to illuminate violence with meaning. Under sea-strange light these little houses glimmer in memory, powerful as radium." Under the surface are hidden worlds. Things float away, and things wash up.

∧

When I was in college I worked as a maintenance laborer at Minntac in Mountain Iron, a summer job. It was 1975. It paid well. I was in the Agglomerator where four monstrous furnaces rolled taconite fines and bentonite into pellets. The machinery in the taconite plant is larger than the human scale. Each furnace was the size of a train engine and as noisy. Laborers wore earplugs, yellow hard hats, fitted goggles, steel-toed boots, and coveralls. I was in an alienated workforce. That summer, the millwrights went out on a wildcat strike, unauthorized by the union. These workers wanted the same wages as their counterparts in the steel mills. Most of the laborers honored their picket line and did not go to work. Steel imports were coming from Brazil into the United States for the first time, increasing the competition and driving down the price. Within a few weeks, the strike was broken. The corporation sued the workers for lost profits, and they gave in and returned to the plant without having made any gains.

My father had instilled in me a sense of solidarity. Never cross a picket line, he said. I didn't. When the strike was called off, I went back to work. Most shifts, I aimed a high-pressure water hose at the taconite pellets that had fallen off the conveyors to the floor of the plant. By washing down the floor, we were able to prevent a build-up that could stop the conveyor from functioning. Sometimes, there were extra chores. When the furnaces were shut down, and after they had spent some days cooling, we would push wheelbarrows inside the cylindrical interiors and shovel out broken bricks. Other times, on the floor of the plant, we emptied hot pellets from the vent pipes from the furnaces. Red pellets, like live coals, were 1000 degrees, and black pellets, 400 degrees. The vents weren't supposed to accumulate hot pellets, but they did. We had thick asbestos suits and gloves for the task. We opened the door at the bottom of the vent pipe and let the pellets fall out into the bucket of a front-end loader, which would turn and dump them onto a conveyor going out to the loading dock. My coworkers suggested wearing a bandanna around the neck to protect myself from the hot pellets raining down through the catwalks from the upper floors. If a pellet fell into the collar, it would stick in the flesh and cause the skin to bubble and melt. Workers called the burn mark a Minntac brand.

Workers all breathed in the dust of the plant. At the time, we weren't aware that taconite fibers are similar to asbestos fibers. Now, it's known that employees of the taconite mine run a higher risk of contracting mesothelioma. When Meridel Le Sueur was a young writer, radium was thought to be a miraculous element. It was used in cosmetics, toothpaste, and cancer treatments. It was painted on watch dials, poisoning factory workers. Only later was radium determined to be carcinogenic.

We were submerged. The furnaces and conveyors were noisy and created their own wind. The Agglomerator had no windows, and it was hot. The paperback books I tucked in my lunch pail curled up stiff as fallen leaves, darkened by heat and whatever was in the air. After every shift, I showered in the "dry" and though I'd soaped and rinsed thoroughly, I toweled taconite dust from my nostrils and the folds of my ears and behind my knees. Grease and dust stained my coveralls and my underwear. Once the whistle blew ending the shift, men drove to the bars and poured beer down their throats. They blacked out, and in oblivion, after the bars closed, drove erratically on side roads to one of the many lakes, chains of lakes, or to the sinuous St Louis River. Some went skinny-dipping, some hooked up with partners they couldn't later remember, and some collided with unmovable objects. Off-limits were the tailings ponds and the abandoned mine pits, steep-walled and filled with ice-cold water, cast-off mechanical equipment, and other unknown hazards.

Mining excavations always need tending, even after the supply of ore is gone. The abandoned open pits suffer "water gain" because of the high-water tables and rain. Pumps must be kept running to avoid flooding. The Hector Mine on the Iron Range operated from 1893 to 1953. In 2019, after a heavy rain, the embankment between the old Hector mine pit and the Embarrass River burst. The water from the mine pit tore a ravine 50 feet wide and 25 feet deep. A burnt orange torrent, the color of iron oxidation, poured into the river and went downstream into the Embarrass Lake, Cedar Island Lake, and Lake Esquagama. Septic systems broke and raw sewage was released. Workers needed to remove rocks and gravel to reopen the stream so it could flow again. Even before this, the lakes and rivers had been proven to have high sulfate levels which largely comes from taconite mines in discharge from waste storage. Sulfates cause Manoomin or wild rice to die, eliminating this sacred source of nutrition and sustenance. The Hector Mine spill made things worse.

With its many lakes, streams, and swamps, the Iron Range is adjacent to the Boundary Waters Canoe Area, a wilderness designated by the federal government. Some want to develop copper sulfide mining near the BWCA even though surface storage of waste rock, tailings and copper sulfide-bearing ore creates acid, heavy metals, and sulfates that seep into groundwater and contaminate lakes, streams and rivers. In this region with a three-way continental divide, contamination puts all forms of life at risk.

∧

There's so much weight. Changes are happening every moment. There are unknowns, and there are known things deliberately disregarded or dismissed. Events in the past are often forgotten. Union-busting, strikes, sabotage, and murders are hidden under a shroud of silence. Data about mining accidents and environmental contamination exists, but it isn't general knowledge.

History documents that treaties made with the tribal nations were not followed. Silences have obscured the facts. Eminent domain has been misused against the tribes. Buying land in Minnesota does not mean buying the mineral rights beneath the surface. Minnesota owns 24 percent of the mineral rights in the state, but the rest is owned by private parties, primarily mining corporations (Mesabi Metallics, Keetac, Cleveland Cliffs, and others). Minerals are profitable, and corporations prioritize profits over people, and so roads and communities are demolished to make way for excavation. As the landscape or tonnage (as the corporations refer to it) is removed, maps are redrawn. Against the large-scale mining operations, people's lives begin to diminish.

∧

When the rich iron ore was depleted in northern Minnesota, the underground mines became open-pit mines. Technological developments allowed the industry to use lower-grade ore to make taconite. Now many of the open-pit mines have been depleted. Recently, mine dumps are consumed in what is called scram mining, furthering the metamorphosis of the landscape. When I drive along Highway 169, I see yard signs with the words: We Support Mining, Mining Supports Us. I know, and they know, it's always been a story of boom and bust.

The darkest place on the Iron Range is the deepest place, the underground mine in Soudan, Minnesota. At Level 27, the shaft is 2,341 feet deep and a perpetual 50 degrees Fahrenheit. The buildings of the mine are situated at one the highest points on the Iron Range, with long views of the forest and surrounding land. The ore from the Soudan mine was exceptionally rich. It was unique and had an extra oxygen molecule in its chemical composition. Along the shaft of the mine are stopes, dugout tunnels that contained the ore that was mined. Without a light, one can't see a hand in front of the face. The mine is so dark that a physics lab was temporarily created there to study dark matter, things in the universe that cannot be seen at all, but that are known because of their interaction with gravity. Neutrinos were shot from the Fermi lab near Chicago through the earth and recorded by several tons of specialized equipment down in the mine shaft. The absolute darkness in the mine avoided a skew in the research results caused by protons. According the European Council for Nuclear Research (CERN), dark matter outweighs visible matter roughly six to one. It travels in next to no time.

∧

In a stream, according to Thomas F. Waters, fish arrange themselves according to the water temperature, width and depth of the water, slope of ground, and pools and riffles over stones. In our streams, fish swim amidst industrial effluences. We can't let ourselves become so accustomed to this situation that we no longer see it.

People, searching for what feels comfortable, arrange themselves in similar ways. Yet we get displaced, intentionally or not. When it occurs, others might signal that we don't belong, or we just feel that way ourselves. Displacement can be temporary or permanent. It occurs in large contexts like climate change, war or violence, natural disasters, or other ways. It also occurs in smaller, individual contexts. We live in complex social systems and ecosystems. There are thousands of variables. Change is hard, but it can sharpen our attention and raise our awareness of what is happening in the environment.

Tensions in the landscape are part of the mosaic. It's all fluid. I'm struck by how often change has wave patterns. A disturbance in one place causes disturbances in other places. Science tells us when waves come into shore, they bounce back: reflection. Waves that slow down and change direction: refraction. When waves bend: diffraction with shadow zones. When waves affect each other: interference, which can be destructive or positive. The Finnish poet Risto Rasa writes: "Just as one wave swims with another wave/ Across the ocean/ We too survive, supporting each other." My immigrant grandparents had to overcome many obstacles to live, work, and raise a family. Although my mother was born in Minnesota, she was held back in first grade because she did not know enough English. For everybody, change is a set of unpredictable currents that will require endurance, creativity, and connection to a larger community.

In my poems, I want to bring together things that are conflicting, noisy, and beautiful. I want to consider all lives: animal, avian, aquatic, and plant life. The poet Rosmarie Waldrop writes: "When eye and mind are interrupted in the travel, a vertical dimension opens out from the horizontal lines. Suddenly we're reading an orchestral score…. No longer one single voice." Attention and vision, both the individual and collective, are gifts that will benefit our communities. The disappearance of trees, wildlife, people, languages, clean water and even geology will leave traces inside the body and not only inside our bodies, but in the body of earth, changing the flow of life.

∧

When I was a child staying overnight in my grandmother's house, the pendulum clock struck each hour. I would awaken from sleep not knowing what had broken into my dreams. Even now, I am up at night. Occasionally, I will wake with a Finnish word in mind, like *hetkessä*. It had been spoken at home. It is usually an ordinary word I've remembered although I hadn't understood or had forgotten what it meant. It's like receiving a letter sent from long ago. It's a memory that brings me closer to the family members who have passed. I savor the word's rhythm. Between languages exists a beautiful threshold space, full of nuanced meaning. Like every Finnish word, the stress is on the first syllable. Every letter is pronounced, none are silent. Double consonants are each pronounced, elongating the sound as if it were a note held long, like a dotted quarter note, the dot indicating the need to hold the sound half again as long. I like the quiet of darkness. Outside, moonlight rains on the roads and inside, it washes against a wall. Wind in the tree branches outside makes shadows sway. It's as if I'd been underwater and suddenly surfaced. Each word, each language, is a musical element, expressive of the intuitions and culture of people who came before. One often finds a word exactly when it is needed. *Hetkessä* means *in next to no time*.

∧

Poetry is a language inside the language. In a poem in next to no time, years can collapse. Whole eras can elide into a few lines, or one moment can be forever held still. Poetry has underwater currents or forces. Muriel Rukeyser says "poetry can extend the document" in a footnote to her poems in "The Book of the Dead," a section of her 1938 book titled *U.S. 1*. It is about the Hawks Nest Tunnel disaster in Gauley Bridge, West Virginia, which killed at least 476 coal miners, mostly African American migrant workers, between 1930 and 1935. Her poems incorporate archival material about the mining disaster with lyric intensity. The title alludes to the Egyptian Book of the Dead and the Mayan Book of the Dead, evoking the power and weight of those ancient funerary texts. In this way, the form of a poem along with its sound patterns, images, associations, and metaphors can bring together the said and unsaid. On a page, a poem has empty spaces that can be understood like the negative space in a drawing. Stanza breaks might be viewed as bends or turns in a river. Line endings in a poem form a shoreline to launch from and land upon, an empty and wave-washed beach, an edge where we can hold the losses and make new paths, where we search and find things new.

Works Cited

Anttonen, Veikko. "The Sampo as a Mental Representation of the Mythic Origin of Growth." Essay. In *Mythic Discourses: Studies in Uralic Traditions*, edited by Frog, Anna-Leena Siikala, and Eila Stepanova. Helsinki: Finnish Literature Society, 2012.

Dayton, Tim. *Rukeyser's The Book of the Dead.* University of Missouri Press, 2003. (Pbk edition, 2015).

"Hill of Three Waters or the Triple Divide." Historical Marker Database. Information collected in partnership with the Cleveland-Cliffs Foundation. https://www.hmdb.org/m.asp?m=27715

"Hull-Rust Mahoning Mine Pit Overlook Historical Marker." Historical Marker Database. Information collected in partnership with the Cleveland-Cliffs Foundation. https://www.hmdb.org/m.asp?m=6776.

Laine, Mary. "Lake Vermilion–Soudan Underground Mine State Park." MNopedia. Minnesota Historical Society. www.mnopedia.org/place/lake-vermilion-soudan-underground-mine-state-park.

Lamppa, Marvin G. *Minnesota's Iron Country: Rich Ore, Rich Lives*. Duluth, MN: Lake Superior Port Cities, 2004.

Le Sueur, Meridel. *Ripening: Selected Work*. Edited by Elaine Hedges. CUNY, NY: Feminist Press, 1990.

Mechthild, and Lucy Menzies. *The Revelations of Mechthild of Magdeburg (1210–1297): Or, The Flowing Light of the Godhead*. Mansfield Centre, CT: Martino Publishing, 2012.

Niedecker, Lorine. Editor, Jenny Penberthy. *Lorine Niedecker: Collected Works*. "(L.Z.)" poem. Berkeley, CA: University of California Press, 2004.

Rasa, Risto Olavi. *Tuhat purjetta: Kootut runot*. [*A Thousand Sails: Collected Poems*]. Helsinki: Otava, 1992 (4th Edition, 2007).

"Underground Lab Open for Business." *CERN Courier*. CERN: The European Organization for Nuclear Research, April 3, 2019. www.cerncourier.com/a/underground-lab-open-for-business.

Waldrop, Rosmarie. *Dissonance (If You Are Interested)*, p 227. Tuscaloosa, AL: University of Alabama Press, 2005.

Waters, Thomas F. *Wildstream: A Natural History of the Free-Flowing River*. St. Paul, MN: Riparian Press, 2000.

Notes

In the Water

"Water-Filled Mine Pit" is an ekphrastic prose poem for the "Mine Songs" music and aerial images created by Sara Pajunen. The poem was also inspired by poet and journalist Meridel Le Sueur: "Let yourself down, as if underwater, into these lost walls, to hunt for treasure, to illuminate violence with meaning. Under sea-strange light these little houses glimmer in memory, powerful as radium."

Surface Displacements

The epigraph by Lorine Niedecker is from her poem, "(L.Z.)," which originated from correspondence with poet Louis Zukofsky.

Three Rivers and the "Surface Displacements" poem refer to the three-way continental divide located in Hibbing, Minnesota, on the Mesabi Iron Range. The watersheds and rivers travel into the Great Lakes, the Mississippi River, and Hudson Bay.

A historical marker at the edge of the Hull-Rust Mahoning mine pit marks the Hill of Three Waters, or the Triple Divide. According to the Historical Marker Database (www.hmdb.org):

> A triple point, or triple divide, is the place where two continental divides intersect and water drains into three different watersheds. There are five such places in the United States. In Minnesota, the Northern Divide intersects the St. Lawrence Seaway Divide.

From this point, water flows in three directions, north to Hudson Bay, south to the Gulf of Mexico, and east to the Gulf of St. Lawrence. This area was called the Hill of Three Waters by the Chippewa, and its location is 47° 26.863' N, 92° 56.8' W. The marker is near Hibbing, Minnesota, in St. Louis County. The Chippewa Indians referred to the location as "The Hill of Three Waters" or "The Top of the World" and frequently held their council meetings there for tribes living within about a 100-mile radius. The site is not publicly accessible due to mining operations. Its official platting is Section 26, Township 58, Range 21.

The Historical Marker Database is a catalog of public history cast in metal, carved on stone, or embedded in resin. The database is maintained by volunteers who invite people to send in photographs and links related to historical markers.

A second historical marker is placed nearby this one at the Hull-Rust Mahoning Mine Pit Overlook. Here the marker notes that mining began in 1895 and this mine pit was once known as the largest open pit mine in the world. Its maximum depth was 600 feet in the Scranton Pit. By 2000, nearly 2 billion tons of iron ore and waste were removed. Both sources note this information is provided in partnership with the Cleveland-Cliffs Foundation. Cleveland-Cliffs is a mining corporation.

"A river catches herself as she is falling" is inspired by the mystic Mechthild von Magdeburg (1207–1282), a Beguine.

"In the city are those who cannot be traced..." is an ekphrastic poem for visual art by Cecilia Ramón. The poem refers to

Argentina's Dirty War (in Spanish, *Guerra Sucia*), also called *Process of National Reorganization, Spanish Proceso de Reorganización Nacional*, or *El Proceso*. As many as 30,000 people were killed or disappeared.

"In their wake, the undocumented…" refers to immigrants who are stowaways inside the hold of planes and ships and those who risk perilous passage over water. The phrase also refers to those who are brought across the borders in secret, inside closed freight trucks and vans.

Three Rivers

In the prose poem "Soliloquy," the sentence *I realize the way my eyes deceive me* echoes a line from the country song "Paper Roses," written and composed by Fred Spielman and Janice Torre. Loretta Lynn and several other country singers have performed and recorded it.

"Dialectics" is a cento. The italicized phrases are taken from Hegel and Marx, whose writings are now available in the public domain.

"Broken Shell" is a retelling of the creation story in the epic poem of Finland, the *Kalevala*, that was performed by traveling minstrels or singers prior to being written down by Elias Lönnrot. Some of the runos, or poems, have never been in print. Beside creation stories, it has magic charms, laments, advice, stories, and adventures.

Otherworld

The Finnish language poems were written while I was at Arteles in Hämeenkyrö, Finland, at the Enter Text residency.

According to Veikko Anttonen in *Mythic Discourses*, in the *Kalevala*, Pohjola refers to the Otherworld and "can take the form of Pohjola (the northland), the womb, a burial ground, a forest, a grave, Tuonela or Manala (underworld or realm of the dead), a strange village or country." He also writes:

> In [Finnish and Uralic] folk narratives, Pohjola is described as a mythic island in the primeval sea, surrounded by open waters. In addition Pohjola is separated from the world of the living by the River of Pohjola, the River of Tuonela, the chasm of Manala, the age-old brook of Manala. The River of Tuonela is the boundary between this world and the other, where everything is reversed in relation to the world of the living.

"Viisitoista Runo / Poem 15" is an ekphrastic poem. Askeli Gallen-Kallela's painting, *Lemminkäinen Äiti*, vividly depicts the story about a woman who brings her son back to life from the river of death. Lemminkäinen is an adventure-loving braggart and mythic hero in the *Kalevala*.

"Kuppi Jäkälä / Cup Lichen" is inspired by a poem of the same title by Helvi Juvonen (1919–1959). She was a Finnish writer and recipient of the Eino Leino Prize in 1957.

Headwaters

The poem "Ghazal: Without Sinking" refers to the music of Hildur Guðnadóttir, an Icelandic composer and cellist.

In the poem "Luck," "A Case of You" refers to the song by Joni Mitchell.

Acknowledgments

I'd like to thank these literary magazines and anthologies for publishing the following poems:

"Four Stones" and "Levels" were published in the *Thunderbird Review*, April 2022.

"No Other Morning like This" was published in *Bringing Joy: A Local Literary Welcome*, an anthology of poems and writing celebrating the work of the twenty-third United States Poet Laureate, Joy Harjo. Copyright 2021 by Fond du Lac Tribal and Community College.

"Water Filled Mine Pit" was recorded by Wisconsin Public Radio as part of the Writers Read program at Northland College and is published in *Re-Wilding*, *Split Rock Review*, 2020.

In the poem, "Surface Displacements," the section that begins "On foot. On the span..." was published in *Rock & Sling*, Volume 10.2.

Surface Displacements, six sections, formerly numbered #8: "A blueprint...," #12: "Here, a sketch of shore...," #17: "In the city are those who cannot be traced...," #18: "My hand disappears over the horizon...," and #24: "Inside the fallen trunks..." were published in *The Laurel Review Chapbook Finalist Folio*, Winter 2019.

"Dialectics" was published in *Undocumented: Great Lakes Poets Laureate*, edited by Ron Riekki and Andrea Scarpino, Michigan State University Press, 2019.

"Joki/River," "Katsoa/To Look," "Hämähakki/Spider," "Kieli/Tongue," "Lautasen/Plates," "Sammal/Moss," "Kuppi Jäkälä/Cup Lichen," "Talvi/Winter," "Revontulet/Aurora Borealis," and "Kengät/Shoes" from the section Otherworld were published in the anthology *Writers on the Edge*, Precipice Collective, 2019.

"Horses" was published under the title "Variations on a Theme: Horses" as a creative nonfiction essay in *Entropy*, the online magazine, on April 12, 2019, www.entropymag.org/variations-on-a-theme-horses.

"Strange Beasts" was published in *Write to the River — Fall 2019: Special World Rivers Edition*, an online publication of Friends of the Mississippi River, www.fmr.org/writetotheriver/fall2019.

"Map / The Way Back" was published in the *Deep Waters* issue of the *Split Rock Review*, November 2018.

"Not Drowning" was part of the Mill City Requiem media art installation at Northern Spark Festival, Minneapolis, in 2016. The work was also available online.

"Soliloquy" was published in *Unbroken Journal*, October 2018.

"St Louis River Route" was recorded by WDSE Playlist as part of the *One River Many Stories* project in 2017.

In addition, I gratefully acknowledge the help and support I've received for this project that has been funded by grants from the State of Minnesota Arts Board, the Finlandia Foundation, and the Arrowhead Regional Arts Council.

I also want to especially thank Julie Gard, Darci Schummer, and Sun Yung Shin for providing feedback and editing assistance in earlier drafts of this book. Thank you to Daniel K. Haataja for his insight, passion, and depth of knowledge about the Finnish language. Thank you to Valerie Stoehr for providing thoughtful observations and a very thorough edit of the final manuscript. Thank you to Catherine Meier for consultation about the cover design. Thank you to Kathy McTavish for doing a close reading, offering editing suggestions from the perspective of a musician and composer, and for designing the book.

About the Author

Sheila Packa is a poet and writer living in Minnesota. She has an MFA in Creative Writing from Goddard College and has taught creative writing and composition at Lake Superior College. She leads poetry and creative writing workshops in community settings and often performs her work in music and media installations with her creative partner Kathy McTavish. She received a 2020 Minnesota State Arts Board Artist Initiative award for poetry, a fellowship from Finlandia Foundation National in 2016, two Loft McKnight Artist Fellowship awards (in poetry and in prose), a Loft Mentor award, and fellowships and grants from the Arrowhead Regional Arts Council. She has four books of poetry and edited the book *Migrations*, an anthology of Lake Superior writers. She served as Duluth's Poet Laureate in 2010–2012. Helsinki composer Olli Kortekangas used four of her poems for "Migrations," a cantata for mezzosoprano and male voice choir, which was premiered by the Minnesota Orchestra in 2016. The recording *Sibelius: Kullervo Kortekangas: Migrations: Minnesota Orchestra: Vänskä* is available through BIS Records. For more information, go to www.sheilapacka.com.

Wildwood River Press

Founded in 2008, Wildwood River Press is a confluence of the arts. This artist-run collaborative creates cross-media exhibitions and live performances. We publish creative work on the web and in print using open-source tools.

This book is available in print, on the web (HTML/CSS), and as an ebook (PDF). It was produced from a single code base filtered through community-created tools made available through the World Wide Web Consortium.

This book is set in Crimson Pro. It is based on the Crimson face by Sebastion Kosch, a serif typeface released under the Open Font License. Crimson was influenced by older fonts such as Minion, Garamond, and others. Crimson was later redesigned by Jacques Le Bailly and released in January 2019. Crimson Pro is currently available in sixteen styles and variable fonts. The typeface is ideal for online environments and long-form texts where readability is key.

CPSIA information can be obtained
at www.ICGtesting.com
Printed in the USA
BVHW071733200922
647266BV00003B/10